CYM WRTH FONCIO

LEARN WELSH WHILE YOU BONK

Stephen Owen Rule

Hunan-gyhoeddwyd gyda hawlfraint
© 2022 gan Stephen Rule

Cedwir pob hawl. Ni chaniateir ailgyhoeddi neu ddefnyddio unrhyw ran o'r llyfr hwn mewn unrhyw fodd heb ganiatâd perchennog yr hawlfraint ar wahân i ddyfyniadau mewn adolygiad llyfr. Am ragor o wybodaeth, cyfeiriad e-bost:
ste_cymru_14@hotmail.com.

Argraffiad llyfr / e-lyfr cyntaf: Mawrth 14fed 2022
ISBN: 9798422469628
Dyluniad y clawr gan Stephen Rule

Self-published and copyrighted © 2022 by Stephen Rule

All rights reserved. No part of this book may be reproduced or used in any manner without written permission of the copyright owner except for the use of quotations in a book review. For more information, email address: ste_cymru_14@hotmail.com.

First paperback / e-book edition: 14th March 2022
ISBN: 9798422469628
Cover design by Stephen Rule

CYMRAEG WRTH FONCIO
LEARN WELSH WHILE YOU BONK

Unfortunately, Welsh is better known for being 'the language of the heavens' rather than 'the language of love' – which doesn't really bode well for this book. However, it's no secret that us Welsh 'do the dirty' too, so here are a few phrases to *Cymraeg-ify* your bedroom time.

Face it, everyone's first port of call after buying a new Welsh-English dictionary is the naughty words. Well, maybe not *everyone*, but it almost certainly is for any learner choosing this book. Perhaps surprisingly, the Welsh word for *sex* (**rhyw**) only comes up once in the whole list of phrases herein. **Rhyw** can also mean '*some*' too (**rhyw ddydd** = *someday*, **rhywbeth** = *something*) so context is key when using this gem in the real world.

This format is of this book is based on the above example in that each entry includes a tame explanation of the phrase so one can use the phrases – or not-so-naughty variations of them – in not-so-naughty situations too. This is primarily for those who don't possess a one-track-mind 99% of the time and who actually care as much about acquiring Welsh as they crave coitus.

The phrases are set out in three sections: *before*, *during* and *after*.

Howsoever you end up using this book, make sure it's as close to hand as that box of Kleenex on your bedside table.

CYN
Before

Faset ti'n licio cael rhyw efo fi heno?

Would you like to have sex with me tonight?

This is a direct translation of the phrase made infamous by Lady Marmalade; *Voulez-vous coucher avec moi ce soir?*). I'm more than happy to admit that this one doesn't have the same ring in Welsh.

I've included **licio** for '*to like*' here for two reasons; one, because it's becoming more and more common to use than **hoffi**, and two, because it sounds like '*lick*' and that's kind of a sexy word.

<u>**Faset ti'n licio...?**</u> is a common phrase heard in non-sexy situations too; like '**faset ti'n licio <u>llefrith?</u>**' (*<u>would you like (some) milk?</u>*). Actually, that one could be twisted too... in a weird and twisted kind of way! I'm not here to judge.

Methu aros cael ti adre' nes ymlaen

Can't wait to have you home later on

Methu actually means *'to fail'* but it's commonly heard instead of the mouthful (pun intended) that is '**ddim yn gallu**' (*not able to; cannot*). Use it in phrases like '**dw i methu mynd**' (*I can't go*) or '**dw i methu credu hynny**' (*I can't believe that*).

Cael is another great verb. It means *'have'* here but it's never used to show possession. It can also mean *'get'* which yields a slightly different meaning in the above sentence.

Finally, it can be used to express *'to get to'* as in *to be allowed to* do something; **Ydw i'n cael mynd?** (*Am I allowed to go?*)

Wnei di helpu fi ddad-sipio?

Will you help me unzip?

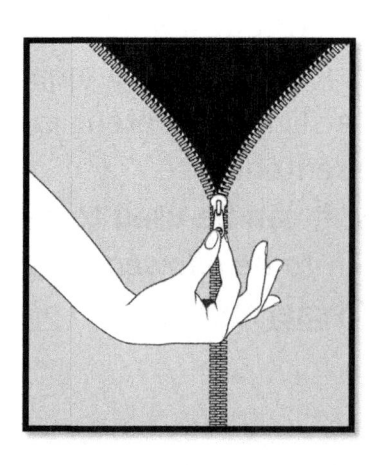

Speaking of unzipping, the term **'wnei di...?'** – second person singular future tense of **'gwneud'** (*to do*) – is a fantastic one to know. It equates to *'will you...?'* in English and is used commonly in Welsh to ask people to *do* stuff for you. Add softly mutated verbs after it like '**wnei di stopio siarad?**' (*will you stop talking?*) or '**wnei di gau'r drws?**' (*will you shut the door?*) to make your alone time that little bit more special.

D(d)at- or **d(dad)-** is often fixed to verbs to equate to *un-* or *dis-* in English; **datgymalu** = *to dislocate*... something worth guarding against in the bedroom, of course.

Mae gynnon ni fatres newydd...

We've got a new mattress...

Who hasn't used this excuse to lie back and think of England [sic]? **Mae gynnon ni** is more commonly heard as '**mae 'da ni**' in the south, with '**mae gennym ni**' more of a literal and 'posh' phrase.

You'll notice that '**matres**' has experienced a soft mutation – coincidentally the same thing that'll happen to one's actual mattress following continued use in a given manner.

Golau ymlaen neu wedi diffodd?

Lights on or off?

Plenty of light to be shed on this phrase too – whether you prefer lights on or off!

Ymlaen can also suggest *'forwards'* or *'onwards'*, whereas **'diffodd'** literally means *'to extinguish'* or *'to eradicate'*. Commonly, Welsh speakers will use the English words *'**on**'* and *'**off**'* because, well, we're a bit lazy at times.

Rarely too lazy for what immediately follows this question, mind.

Oes gen ti amddiffyniad?

Have you got protection?

Listen up uni' students and festival goers, this sentence is for you!

From the word **'amddiffyn'** (*to protect; to defend*), the suffix **'-iad'** is often added to verbs to form nouns; **caru** (*to love*) > **cariad** (*a love(r)*), **taflu** (*to throw*) > **tafliad** (*a throw, a fling*), **mesur** (*to measure*) > **mesuriad** (*a measure(ment)*).

With a bit of imagination, each of those examples could be used in the bedroom.

Dy dro di ar dop, 'dydy?

Your turn on top, isn't it?

I largely chose this one for its æsthetic alliteration. To be fair, '*on top*' would best be translated as '**ar y pen**', but this could be confused with '*at the top/head/end.*'

Having said that, no reason why both couldn't be utilised and appropriated for a couple's special time!

The tag "**dydy?**" derives from '**onid ydy(w)?**' and is the common equivalent of '*isn't it?*' or, for the cool folk, '*i'nit?*')

Rhaid i ti agor y bronglwm 'ma!

You'll have to open / unhook this bra!

Rhaid i ti (*you must*) isn't a common one in the bedroom, but no partner has ever had 100% success rate with regards to this sentence and has certainly asked for aid on at least one occasion. Fact.

Substitute **'i ti'** for **'i fi,' 'iddo fo,' 'iddi hi,' 'i ni' 'i chi'** or **'iddyn nhw'** (*[to/for] me, he, she, we, you (plural/formal), they respectively*) to make phrases useful outside the bedroom too.

In other news, the word **bronglwm** is made from **'bron'** (*boob*) and **'clymu'** (*to tether up*). Ouch!

Dw i isio sboelio ti heno ('ma)

I want to spoil you this evening

Dw i isio (spotted/heard as '**dw i mo'yn**' in southern reaches of Wales) is one of those structures everyone should know. Armed with that, '**bore da**' and '**diolch**', why would any untrained ear believe that you weren't just another fluent speaker in a shop?

Sboelio is simply lifted straight from English. However, the suffix '**-io**' suggests a verb – it can't be used to make every single word 'Welsh' as some like to believe. *Fourio* is not how one says '**pedwar**' in Welsh! However, one might actually hear '*sixty-nine-io*', I guess.

Cyfle am *jwmp* heno?

Fancy / Chance of a jump *tonight?*

Ok, this one's just downright vulgar. Unsurprisingly common in south-western Wales - dirty beggars! - it's simply a Welshier version of *'jump'*; a term often used in French (*niquer*) to refer to a one-nighter.

Cyfle is a *'chance at'* or an *'opportunity for'* and is often followed by **am**. Many use '**siawns**' (and Welshified version of the English word) too. Fancy your chances at getting lucky?

WRTHI
During

NB: **Wrthi** is probably best translated as 'at it' here; hence my choosing it. *During* (in the 'normal' sense) is **yn ystod**.

Fel yna!

Like that!

Simple and to the point... literally. Also heard outside Welsh bedrooms in phrases such as '**dw i isio un fel yna**' (*I want one like that*) and '**oes gen ti un fel yna?**' (*have you got one like that?*)

One might also wish to add '**(yn) union**' before a phrase like this for more effect and to express '*exactly*' or '*just*'; **union fel yna** (*just like that*). Dropping the initial '**yn**' shouldn't really be done, but in the frantic heat of the moment etc...

Yna is often shortened to '**na** and, coupled with **y(r)** (= *the*), is how we express *that [something]*; eg **y ci 'na** (*that dog*), **y llyfr 'na** (*that book*).

Paid stopio!

Don't stop!

Paid, meaning *don't*, can also be seen as **peidiwch** (formal, plural form) and often followed by 'â.' **Peidiwch â rhedeg!** (*Don't run!*), **Paid (â) mynd yno!** (*Don't go there!*).

Plenty of non-Welshies believe that you can just chuck -io at the end of any word in Welsh and get away it. Wrong! You can only do it with verbs – or, essentially, pretty much any word to which you can add -ing in English. **Parcio** = *to park, parking*, **marcio** = *to mark, marking*, **cario** = *to carry, carrying*, etc.

Wyt ti isio newid safle?

Do you want to change position?

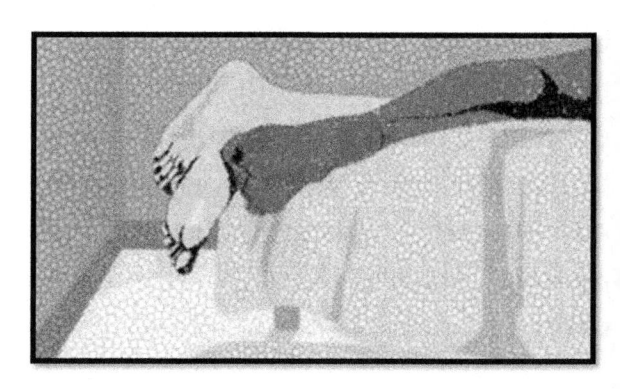

Wyt ti? can express both *do you?* and *are you?* making it a tidy little one to know if you're starting to brave the realms of actually conversing with people in Welsh. Remember that '-ing' is free in Welsh (eg **isio** is *to want* AND *wanting*) so **dw i isio** can be both *I [do] want* and *I am wanting*.

Newid is a great word to know because, aside from its clear and obvious usefulness in everyday life, it's also the same word for '*change*' in both the verb and noun form – something much rarer in Welsh than in English. One might say '**ga' i newid fy nillad?**' (*can I change my clothes?*) as well as '**dyma dy newid**' (*here's your change*).

Safle translates literally as '*a place where one stands.*' Welsh sex is best!

Sut mae hynny i ti?

How's that for you?

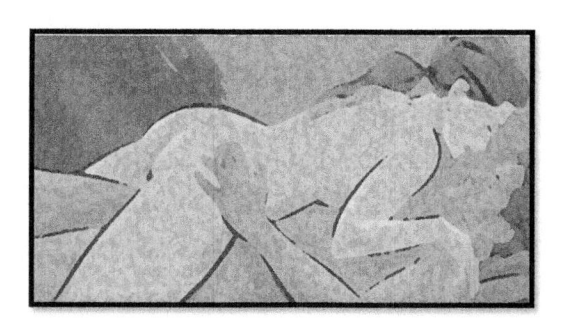

It's always nice to be considerate, right? This one tends to only be asked when, deep down, the asker is pretty certain what they're doing at that moment will yield a positive response.

'**Sut mae?**' (*How is it? / How be it?*) is found as a standalone phrase equivalent to the English '*hi*' or '*alright?*' In northern dialects, it's shortened to '**s'mae?**' whereas southerners tend to go for '**shw'mae?**' – **sut** having changed to '**shw(t)**'.

'**Hynny**' (along with '**hwnnw**', '**honno**' and other dialectal variations) is used to express the pronoun 'that'. **Dw i'n licio <u>hynny</u>** = *I like that*, **Ga' i <u>hynny</u>?** = *May I have that?*

Mae o mor fawr!

It's so big!

I'll tell you what's big... knowing how to express *'it'* in Welsh. Technically we should be using '**hi** or **o** (**e** in southern dialects) after working out whether the thing to which we're referring as *'it'* is a feminine or masculine word. I've gone for the masculine version in the above sentence for absolutely no reason at all... honest! These days people just use whatever they want and sometimes even leave it out completely; '**www, dw i'n licio!**' (*ooo, I like [it]!*).

I've used the northern version of *'it'* here (**o** instead of **e**) because, well, you're more likely to hear this phrase as a northern bloke than a southern one... Yeah, I went there!

Mor is actually a really useful word too because it can double the number of ways you can describe things. Whack it before any adjective – remembering your soft mutation – and away you go; **dw i mor drist** (*I'm so sad*), **roedd hi mor dda** (*it/she was so good*).

Cyflymach! Caletach!

Faster! Harder!

I'll be the first to admit that the '**ch**' sound in Welsh isn't the most romantic of sounds, but you won't get far using superlatives in Welsh without it. Want to add '**-er**' to your adjectives? This one's for you! **Araf<u>ach</u>** (*slow<u>er</u>*) and **dyfn<u>ach</u>** (*deep<u>er</u>*) might also be of aid in sexy situations but, with a couple of exceptions, the suffix '**-ach**' can be added to all adjectives in Welsh.

Dw i wir yn agos!

I'm really close!

For most starting out learning, **iawn** means *okay*, *alright*. It's usually the response I get once 'happy time' is over! Many learners are also aware that popping a **iawn** after an adjective doubles as *'very'*; **boddhaol iawn** (*very satisfactory*), **siomedig iawn** (*very disappointing*).

Wir, on the other hand, translates as *'true,'* but, as in the above sentence, is often used to express *'really'* too once an **yn** follows it.

Ydy o mewn eto?

Is it in yet?

There are two ways to express *'in'* in Welsh. The definite way; **yn** (the very same one that causes those nasty nasal mutations) and the indefinite way; **mewn**. This phrase uses a more common version of **'i mewn'** (*inside*). The initial **'i'** is as optional as asking the question in the first place, hence hurting your partner's feelings.

One might also wish to respond to this question with the phrase on the previous page. If that doesn't help, then I certainly can't help you!

Paid [di] â meiddio rhoi o yna!

Don't [you] dare put it (in) there!

Paid [â] (= *do not*) is common because no one behaves themselves in Wales! Many leave out the '**â**' in speech, but it 'should' be there. My native-speaking wife often adds a '**di**' (*you*) in there for added emphasis on whatever it is now that I shouldn't be doing.

Meiddio is from **beiddio** meaning *to dare* or *to defy*. I have as much idea of why it experiences a nasal mutation here as I do in knowing where to put certain things. It's 50/50, for crying out loud. I didn't mean to!

In other news, **rhoi** can also mean *to give*… so, yeah, that might come in handy too!

Mae hynny'n anhygoel!

That's incredible!

It's always nice to commend one's partner on a job well done and there aren't many better things to hear than this. Substitute **'anhygoel'** for any adjective to describe anything you like; nude or otherwise.

Much like its English equivalent *'incredible; unbelievable'*, the word **'anhygoel'** can also be used in an almost sarcastic manner to describe something, well, not so *'incredible'*, really. Speakers also add 'o' after it to express the adverb *'incredibly'* too; **anhygoel o wael** (*incredibly bad*) or **anhygoel o dda** (*incredibly good*).

AR ÔL
After

Diolch yn fawr iawn

Thanks a lot

There's always time for manners. A phrase common across Wales and understood by... well, everyone, really.

Don't just confine this one only until just before you've sparked up your cigarette in bed! There's no excuse to use anything else to thank people in Wales - Welsh speakers or otherwise.

Oww, da iawn ti!

Aww, well done you!

If you received any part of your education in Wales, you're probably well-versed with this one. What few people know is that, as well as meaning '*well done*', it also suggests '*very good*'. Grammatically, in fact, recognising **da** as *good* (as in **bore da**, **p'nawn da**, etc) plus **iawn** (which, when following an adjective, means *very*), *very good* is probably a better translation.

Side note for the gents: Do not despair… hearing this phrase really isn't as patronising as it sounds. I hear it all the time and I've been told first-hand that partners really do mean it sincerely.

Wyt ti 'di gorffen?

Have you finished?

For him and her; but more likely for her, right? Outside sound-proof walls, this one's great in many situations and is one people might remember from their school days.

'Di, often shortened in speech from **wedi**, is the past particle in Welsh and, when followed by a verb, creates the English equivalent of *'have done something'* eg **dw i wedi bwyta'n barod** (*I have eaten already*), **maen nhw wedi gweld o** (*they have seen it/him*).

Cofia hynny am y tro nesa'!

Remember that for next time!

Coincidentally, the verb '**cofio**' (*to remember*) is a great one to remember, whether certain antics in one's personal time are memorable or not. Here it's changed to '**cofia**' which is a less formal way of giving a command in Welsh; the more formal suffix being **-wch**. eg **sbïa** (*look* - informal request); **sbïwch** (*look* - formal command or plural).

Roeddet ti ar dân yna!

You were on fire there/then!

Roeddet ti is a bit like **rwyt ti** (*you are*) but in the past tense. It can be shortened to '**ro't ti**' yielding stuff like '**ro't ti'n hapus**' (*you were happy*). In each case, drop the initial **R** to form a question; **oeddet ti?** (*were you?*).

Ar dân can describe something literally *on fire* – **roedd y coed ar dân** (*the trees were on fire*) or, as in this example, as an explanation of how fantastic you are in the sack. Notice how the preposition **ar** (*on*) has caused a soft mutation on **tân** (*fire*)... it does that!

Yna can be used as the term for *there* (as in a place you can see / point at) – **dw i'n gweld hi yna** (*I see her there*), and it can be used as the term to denote a recent time – **yna es i adref** (*then I went home*). Wedyn (then, later, after(wards)) can be substituted for the latter.

Wnes i fwynhau hynny

I enjoyed that

Here's something else to enjoy; forming the simple past tense in Welsh. Though more commonly heard in northern Welsh dialects, using **gwneud** (*to do, to make*) as an auxiliary verb is used and understood across the country.

Wnes i (sometimes shortened to **'nes i**) means '*I did, I made*' which, when placed before a softly mutated verb, forms the simple past tense.

Don't be surprised to see people expressing **mwynhau** (= *to enjoy*) as **joio** in Welsh either.

Oes gen ti hances, plîs?

Have you got a tissue, please?

If you're hearing '**nag oes**' in response to this question then you probably didn't prepare very well…

Just like any **hances**, phrases employing '**oes gen ti…?**' can be used to clean up anyone's messy Welsh. We mentioned '**oes gen ti…?**' earlier. Use it in local coffee shops to ask whether any chocolate cake is available (**oes gen ti gacen siocled ar gael?**) or when asking if someone's got time to see you (**oes gen ti amser i weld fi?**). We should expect a soft mutation on any following noun, but don't worry if you forget because you'll always be understood.

Pryd gawn ni 'neud eto?

When will we get to do it again?

Gawn ni comes from the verb '**cael**' (*to get/to get to*). Here in this case, **gawn ni** suggests *'will we get to'* - a non-sexual example might be '<u>**gawn ni** fynd rŵan?</u>' (*can we go now? will we get to go now?*).

Eto is a cool word because it can mean *'again'* (**dw i'n mynd <u>eto</u>** = *I'm going again*) and *'yet'* (**dw i heb fod <u>eto</u>** = *I haven't been yet*). In a sad twist of events, the fact that *'yet again'* is expressed as '**unwaith <u>eto</u>**' (= *once again*) and not '***eto eto***' represents a huge, missed opportunity in the Welsh language.

Wyt ti'n cysgu'n barod?

Are you sleeping already?

While your beloved sleeps off the effects of your incredible prowess, you can spend your downtime delving into the wonderful world of Welsh adverbs. In English, adverbs are usually created by adding '-*ly*' at the end of an adjective.

Welsh employs a much different but just as simple way; by whacking an '**yn**' before a softly mutated adjective like sloppy smooch mid-coitus.

Examples include:
barod = *ready* > **yn barod** = *already*,
hapus = *happy* > **yn hapus** = *happily*,
swnllyd = *loud* > **yn swnllyd** = *loudly*,
arbennig = *special* > **yn arbennig** = *especially*.

Dw i isio cwtsio rŵan

I want to cuddle now

Now you're done, what better way than to request a sweaty, smelly snuggle in the beautiful language of the heavens? Contrary to popular belief both outside and within Wales' borders, **cwtsh** (or the anglicised '***cwtch***') doesn't mean a *hug* or a *cuddle* everywhere.

Up in the north-east it's regularly used for a *cubby hole* or *hiding place*. The verb, **cwtsio**, is an archaic term for **cuddio** (= *to hide*) in the north too.

Dilynwch Doctor Cymraeg ar Drydar
Follow Doctor Cymraeg on Twitter

@CymraegDoctor

OTHER (NOT-SO-FILTHY YET JUST AS SEXY) BOOKS BY STEPHEN RULE

WELSH WHILE YOU GET P*SSED
ISBN: 9798353362296

WELSH WHILE YOU BONK
ISBN: 9798422469628

CRACKING WELSH QUESTIONS
ISBN: 9798774777815

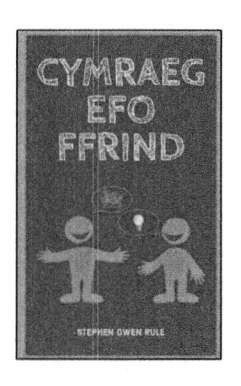

WELSH WITH A FRIEND
ISBN: 9798531490421

THE FORGOTTEN CIRCLE
ISBN: 979804158080

THE SUREXIT SECRET
ISBN: 9798711837435

SAVING CAERWYDDNO
ISBN: 9798717273046

67 FAVOURITE WELSH VERBS
ISBN: 9798364748805

WELSH AND I
ISBN: 9798669438609

GEIRIADUR CYMRAEG-SESOTHO
ISBN: 9798717163989

CELTIC QUICK-FIX
ISBN: 9798585857645

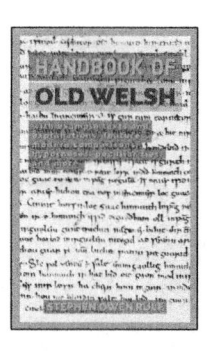

HANDBOOK OF OLD WELSH
ISBN: 9798444225370

PARSNIPS AND OWLS
ISBN: 9798833259184

CORNISH WITH A FRIEND
ISBN: 9798354658381

PARSNIPS AND OWLS 2
ISBN: 9798833259184

CORNISH DIARY
ISBN: 9798544697275